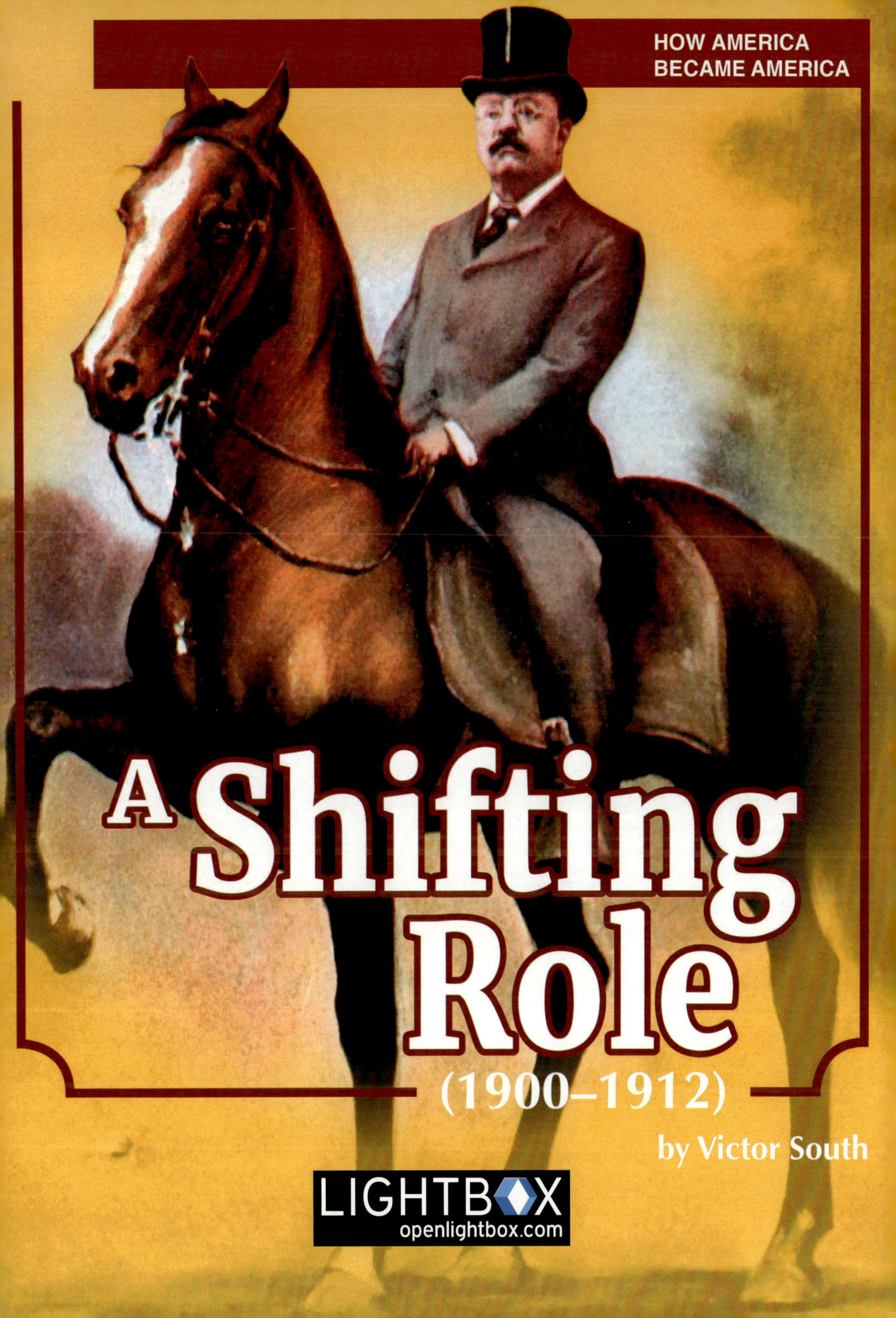

HOW AMERICA BECAME AMERICA

A Shifting Role

(1900–1912)

by Victor South

LIGHTBOX

openlightbox.com

LIGHTBOX

Go to **www.openlightbox.com** and enter this book's unique code.

ACCESS CODE

LBXF3488

Lightbox is an all-inclusive digital solution for the teaching and learning of curriculum topics in an original, groundbreaking way. Lightbox is based on National Curriculum Standards.

STANDARD FEATURES OF LIGHTBOX

AUDIO High-quality narration using text-to-speech system

ACTIVITIES Printable PDFs that can be emailed and graded

SLIDESHOWS Pictorial overviews of key concepts

VIDEOS Embedded high-definition video clips

WEBLINKS Curated links to external, child-safe resources

TRANSPARENCIES Step-by-step layering of maps, diagrams, charts, and timelines

INTERACTIVE MAPS Interactive maps and aerial satellite imagery

QUIZZES Ten multiple choice questions that are automatically graded and emailed for teacher assessment

KEY WORDS Matching key concepts to their definitions

Contents

Chapter One

America's Growing Power

In 1909, 16 gleaming white ships sailed in a parade 7 miles (11 kilometers) long. President Theodore Roosevelt watched proudly from the deck of another boat.

The ships were coming home from a journey around the world. They had stopped in 20 different ports along the way. They landed on six continents.

Together, the ships were called the "Great White **Fleet**." Their journey was Roosevelt's way of telling the world that the United States was a powerful country.

Few people knew of President's Roosevelt's plan for the Great White Fleet when the ships set out. Most people thought the fleet was traveling only from the East Coast to the West Coast.

Many Americans wanted the United States to have a bigger role in the world. Roosevelt agreed. Americans wanted the United States to be great. To them, that meant that the country would get bigger. It had already spread from the Atlantic coast of North America to the Pacific Ocean. Where else could it spread? People started looking across the ocean.

If the United States got bigger, it would be more powerful. It could also bring **democracy** and freedom to new people. The United States would really be doing the world a favor. Or at least that's what Americans told themselves. That way of thinking is called imperialism. It means that a country gains control of more land and builds an **empire**.

About **14,000** sailors and marines took part in the **Great White Fleet's voyage**.

The fleet traveled **43,000 miles** (69,200 km).

The voyage was the **first trip around the world** by a group of steam-powered, steel ships.

MANIFEST DESTINY

At the beginning of the 1800s, the United States was just on the East Coast. But there was room to grow. Americans thought that they should spread out over the whole continent. They believed they had a responsibility to bring democracy to people who didn't have it. They thought God wanted them to do that. That idea was called Manifest Destiny. It was one of the reasons that, during the 1800s, people moved out West and made it all the way to California, Alaska, and Hawai'i.

There were also a lot more people in the United States. They needed room to live. They started moving out West, where there was plenty of land. They ignored the fact that Native Americans already lived there.

At the time that the Great White Fleet sailed, the world's largest empire was the British Empire. In the past, it had included the American **colonies**. The colonies hadn't liked being part of the British Empire. They fought the American Revolutionary War to gain independence and become the United States.

In the early 1900s, not everybody wanted America to build its own empire. Some people thought the United States should mind its own business. It shouldn't try to take over other countries. It should set an example of peace for the rest of the world.

The American Revolutionary War was fought from 1775 to 1783. The colonies' Continental Army was led by George Washington and helped by France during the war.

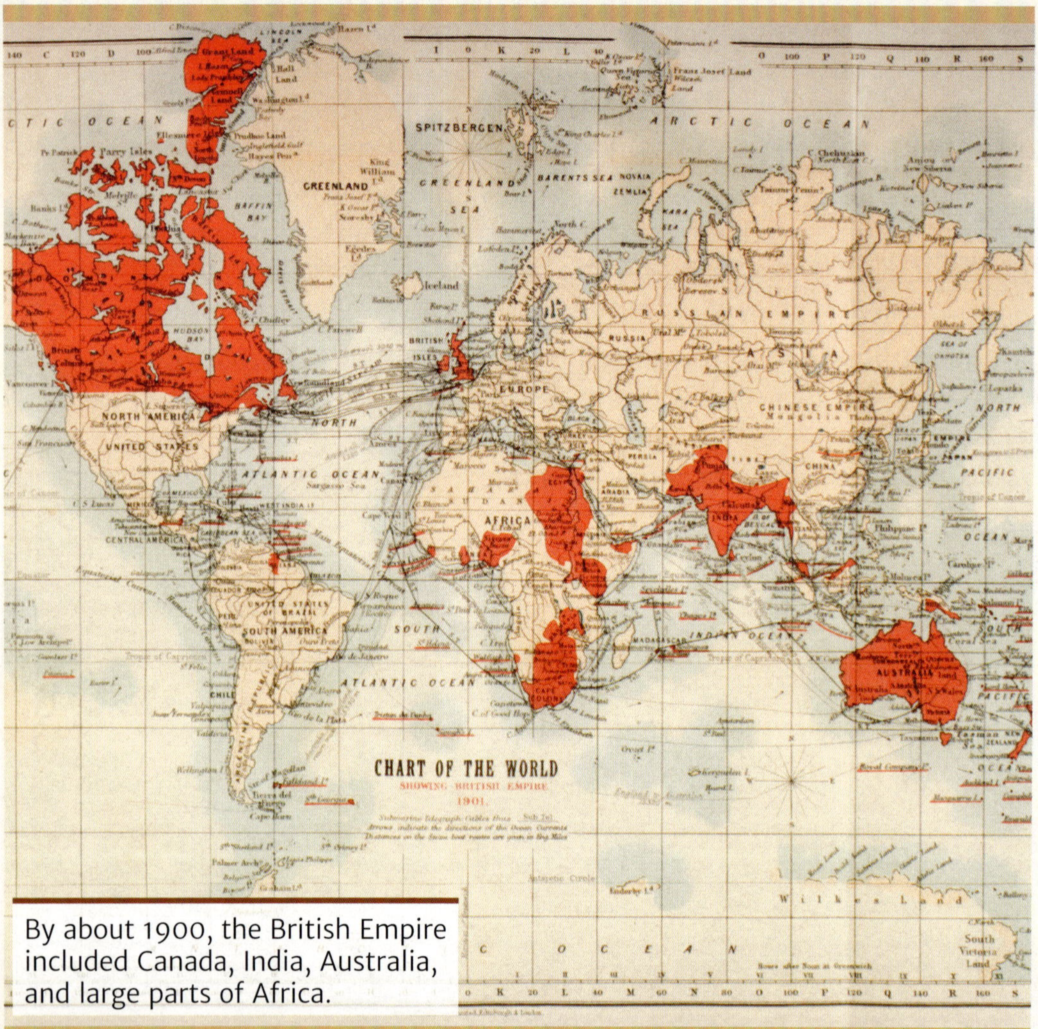

By about 1900, the British Empire included Canada, India, Australia, and large parts of Africa.

THE BRITISH EMPIRE

England started getting more powerful during the 1500s, under Queen Elizabeth I. Her explorers traveled all around the world. They claimed land for England everywhere they went. England joined with Scotland and Wales to become Great Britain in 1707. The British ended up owning a lot of land with a lot of things that could make them money. Furs, gold, food and spices, cotton, and many other items all went to Great Britain. The British created colonies in North America, Africa, Asia, and other places. The power of the British kept growing for a long time.

In the 1890s, Theodore Roosevelt had served as police commissioner of New York City and as governor of New York State.

Before he was president, Theodore Roosevelt worked for the navy. He had always been ready for war, as long as it meant it could make the United States grow. When he became president in 1901, Roosevelt especially wanted to make the navy stronger. A strong fleet of ships would make the United States powerful.

Great Britain's position as the biggest power in the world was already being challenged. Other countries were trying to take over some British colonies. The United States decided it was time to take Britain's place in the world.

GET THINKING

Power and Democracy

In a lot of ways, today's Americans are still facing the same questions that Americans did back in the first years of the 20th century. The United States is a very powerful country. How should it use that power? Should the United States run other countries? Is it okay for it to spread democracy? Is the United States helping other people around the world when it does that? Should American power have a limit?

Chapter Two

The Panama Canal

For a long time, there was no easy way to get from the Atlantic to the Pacific Ocean by boat. Not if you were in North America. You had to sail all the way to the very southern tip of South America. It was a very, very long journey.

The other option was to take your ships apart. Then, you dragged everything across the narrowest part of the Americas, in Central America. After that, you built your ships again.

Then, somebody came up with the idea of a canal. These human-made waterways had been built in other parts of the world, including Europe and Asia. People could build a waterway through a narrow piece of land in Central America. Then, ships could sail straight from one ocean to the other without having to travel extra thousands of miles.

From the 1500s to the early 1800s, Spain had a lot of power in Central America. The Spanish started thinking about building a canal. It would help them out a lot.

In the 16th century, King Charles I of Spain imagined digging a waterway across Central America.

China's Grand Canal, built in the 1300s, is the longest and one of the oldest canals in the world.

First, Spain wanted to build it in Nicaragua. But then Nicaragua became a free country. Spain couldn't build the canal because it didn't control the country any more. But Nicaragua could build it.

The United States was also interested in building a canal. It sent a lot of ships around South America. A canal would be useful for trading and for the military.

American and other vessels traveling around the southern tip of South America often had to sail through storms and rough water.

The first American to think about it may have been Benjamin Franklin, in the late 1700s. But the American Revolutionary War was going on, so there wasn't any time to do anything further. The idea stuck around, though.

The United States looked at a few places to build a canal, with the help of other countries. It looked at Colombia. Then, the United States actually started to build a canal in Nicaragua, but the work didn't get very far.

Meanwhile, the French started building a canal in Panama. But it turned out to be a disaster. There were floods and earthquakes and diseases and accidents. The French gave up. It was too much trouble.

Finally, the United States was ready to really build a canal. American leaders had time to focus on it now. The problem was, the government still didn't know where it wanted to build.

The digging equipment used by the French workers trying to build a canal did not work well in Panama's rocky ground.

There were two choices. A canal could be built in Nicaragua. There was a river and a lake that could help builders. They wouldn't have to build as far.

The other choice was in Panama, where the French had already started. Part of the work was already done.

It was a big argument. Panama started looking like it would be cheaper. But there was still one problem. Panama was owned by Colombia. It wasn't an independent country.

Plans for a canal across Panama included using the Chagres River. However, the many crocodiles in the river were a danger for canal workers.

Colombia was asking for a lot of money from the United States. It didn't just want to let the United States build a canal. It wanted to get something out of it.

Roosevelt never backed down from a challenge. He used to play a game called "obstacle walk." He usually played it with children who came to visit him. The only rule was to get past obstacles by climbing over them. You couldn't go around them.

That's exactly how Roosevelt tackled this problem. He went right over it. He didn't want to pay Colombia. Instead, he would just make Panama into its own country.

The United States helped Panama revolt. The U.S. Army helped. It made sure Colombia could not send soldiers to Panama to prevent the revolt. And Panama became a country in 1903.

Theodore Roosevelt played obstacle walk with his own six children, even when he was president.

Within a month, the United States was in control of a piece of land in Panama. It was called the Canal Zone. It was 10 miles (16 km) wide. The United States could start building.

The deal made a lot of people mad. Not everyone liked what the United States had done. Some Panamanians were angry. They thought the United States had too much control over their country.

Other countries in South America were mad too. Colombia especially didn't like the United States. It had taken away part of its land and people.

But Americans were generally happy. Having a canal would make trading easier. It also showed the world that the United States was becoming more powerful.

Right away, the United States ran into trouble, though. Panama wasn't a very good place to build a canal. France had found that out before. Now, as it started building, the United States would find that out again, the hard way.

People in Panama who wanted the country to be independent held a large demonstration in Panama City in 1903.

The Canal Zone was in the middle of the jungle. It was hot. The people building the canal got sick. Almost 6,000 men died. Most of them had diseases such as yellow fever or malaria.

But they kept at it. It took years to build the canal. In 1914, it was finally finished. Thanks to the United States and others, the Atlantic and Pacific Oceans were linked together.

VASCO NUÑEZ DE BALBOA

Balboa was a Spanish conquistador, or conqueror, during the 1500s. He came to the Americas looking for treasure, but he didn't find any. Balboa ended up on a Caribbean island called Hispaniola. He didn't have any money left, so he tried farming. He failed.

Balboa went to South America. He established one of the first European settlements there. Then, he traveled north into Panama and across Panama to the Pacific Ocean. He crossed jungles and mountains. Balboa is believed to be the first European to reach the Pacific Ocean. He claimed all of the land that he saw for Spain.

Building the Panama Canal

Parts of Panama are mountainous. Instead of cutting through mountains, canal workers built a system to raise and lower ships. The workers created a lake, Gatun Lake, in a mountainous area near Panama's Atlantic coast. Then, they built a series of locks, which are similar to elevators for ships.

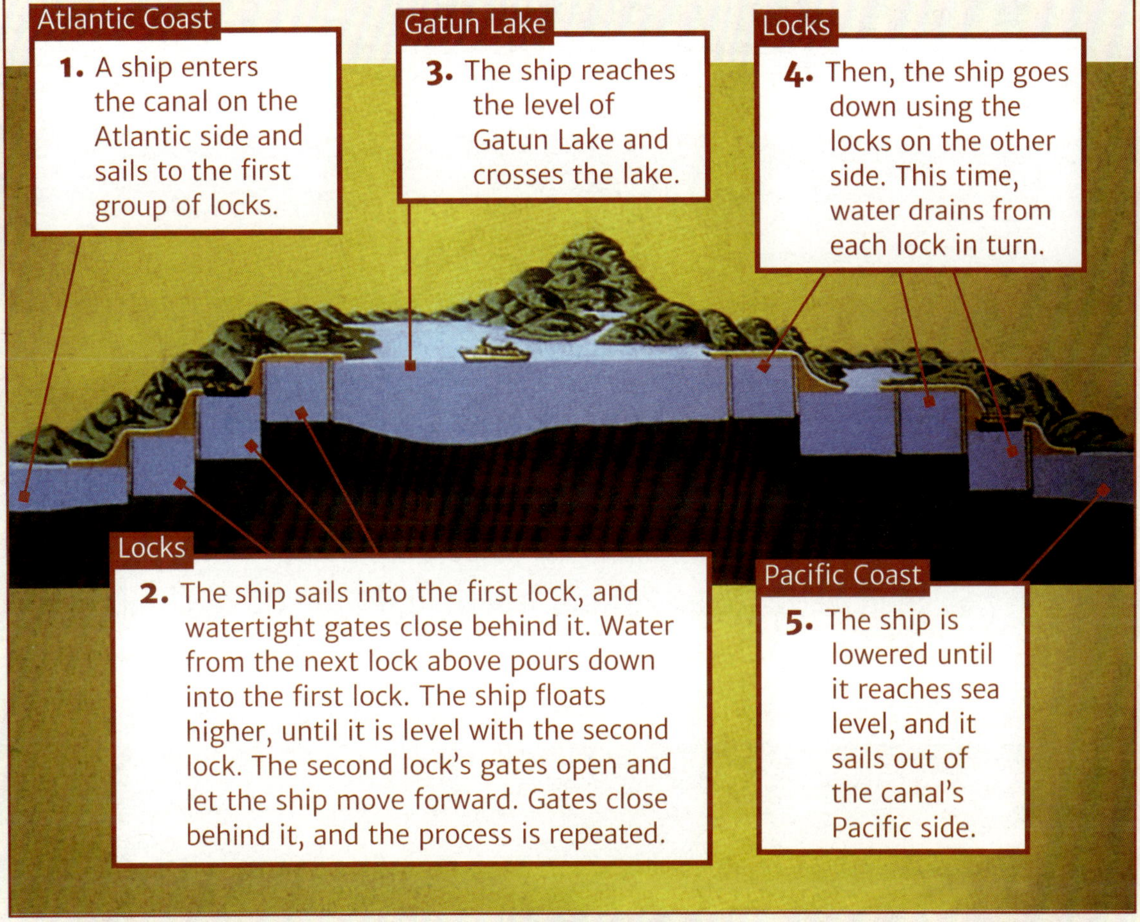

More than **40,000 people** worked on building the Panama Canal.

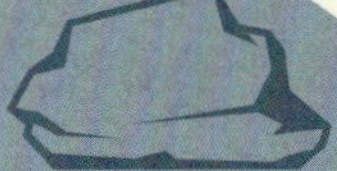

Workers moved more than **268 million cubic yards** (205 million cubic meters) of dirt and rock to dig the canal.

Ships traveling from New York to San Francisco sailed **7,800 miles** (12,550 km) less by using the canal.

Chapter Three

Taking over Latin America

Theodore Roosevelt was a president with a lot of character. Some people loved him, and some people hated him.

Roosevelt did a lot of good things for the United States. He found ways to control huge companies that hurt other companies. He set aside land for national parks. He helped make food safer in the United States.

But Roosevelt also did some not so good things. He made a lot of other countries mad. He believed that Central and South America weren't as good as the United States. He thought the United States had the right to control the people who lived there. And he wasn't afraid to use that right.

President Roosevelt helped create nine national parks. They include Mesa Verde, in Colorado, which features ancient Native American buildings.

Cartoonists of his time made fun of Roosevelt for his statement about carrying a big stick.

Roosevelt liked to say "Speak softly and carry a big stick." He meant that you shouldn't get angry and you should be friendly—but you should also be willing to use your strength to fight enemies.

Roosevelt didn't speak very softly. He did carry a big stick, though. And he wasn't afraid to use it.

In **1906**, Theodore Roosevelt won the **Nobel Peace Prize** for helping end a war between Russia and Japan.

At age 42, Roosevelt was the **youngest person** to become president.

While Roosevelt was president, **230 million acres** (93 million hectares) of land were added to national parks and national forests.

Before Roosevelt's time, the United States wanted to keep Europe out of the Americas. President James Monroe warned Europe not to do anything in the Western Hemisphere. If a European country did, the United States would see it as war. That was called the Monroe Doctrine.

Roosevelt added on his own words to the Monroe Doctrine. He added what is known as the Roosevelt **Corollary**. It said that the United States had the right to keep the peace in the Americas. It basically said that the United States was the boss in all of the Americas. As long as the United States could keep the peace, there was no reason for Europe to get involved.

THE MONROE DOCTRINE

The Monroe Doctrine was stated by President Monroe in 1823. It was a big turning point in how the United States dealt with the outside world. The doctrine said that the United States didn't want Europe interfering with North or South America. The United States would have to use its military if that happened. It also said that the United States wouldn't interfere with Europe.

The United States wanted to have all the power in North and South America. The ideas in the Monroe Doctrine lasted a very long time. Later presidents would use it to explain American actions. But nobody ever asked people in other North or South American countries what they thought.

Where did the corollary come from? It started because of some things that happened in the Dominican Republic. That's a country on the island of Hispaniola in the Caribbean Sea. A man named General Ulises Heureaux became the president of the Dominican Republic in 1882.

Ulises Heureaux fought for the Dominican Republic's independence from Spain in the early 1860s.

Many American-owned farms in the Dominican Republic in the early 1900s grew sugarcane. Harvesting was done by workers using a machete, or large, heavy knife.

People liked Heureaux at first. Then, he became a **dictator**. He didn't give people any freedom. He killed people. He made the country poor, and he owed a lot of money to other countries.

People in the United States owned farms and businesses in the Dominican Republic. The United States could lose a lot of money based on what the Dominican Republic did. The United States decided this was a reason to get involved in the Dominican Republic.

Then, Roosevelt realized it was a reason to get involved in more countries. He didn't want other dictators taking over. The United States could keep things calm. And it could show the world that it was the most powerful country around.

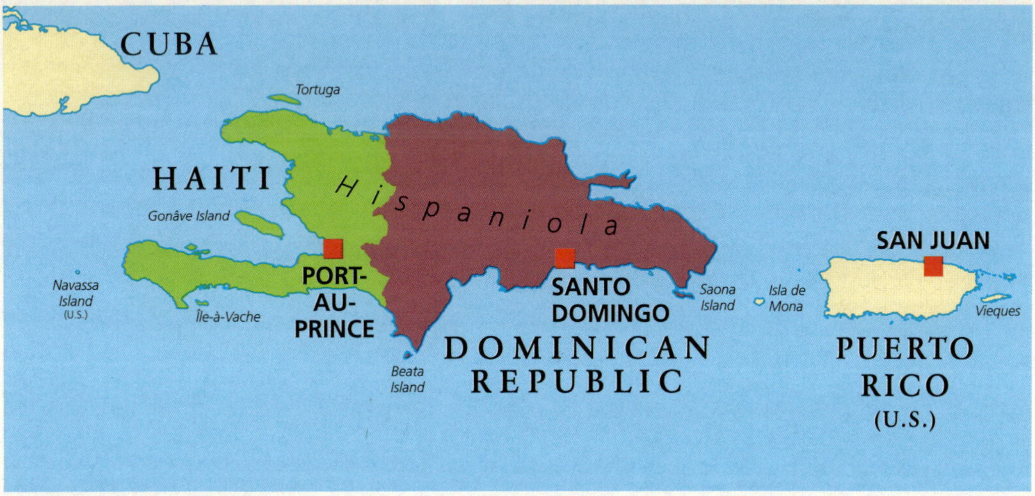

The Dominican Republic covers the eastern part of Hispaniola. The country of Haiti is on the western portion of the island.

With his corollary to the Monroe Doctrine, Roosevelt was mostly concerned about the part of the Western Hemisphere known as Latin America. It includes Mexico, most of Central America and South America, and many Caribbean islands. The term *Latin America* refers to all the areas in the Americas that became colonies of Spain, Portugal, or France. The European colonists brought the Spanish, Portuguese, or French language to those areas. These languages all come from the ancient language Latin, and that is why much of the Western Hemisphere is called Latin America.

Today, almost all of Latin America is made up of independent countries. France still controls French Guiana in South America and a few islands in the Caribbean. Puerto Rico is part of the United States.

Roosevelt stated his corollary in a speech in 1904, shortly before he was reelected and then sworn in for a second term as president at a Washington, D.C., ceremony.

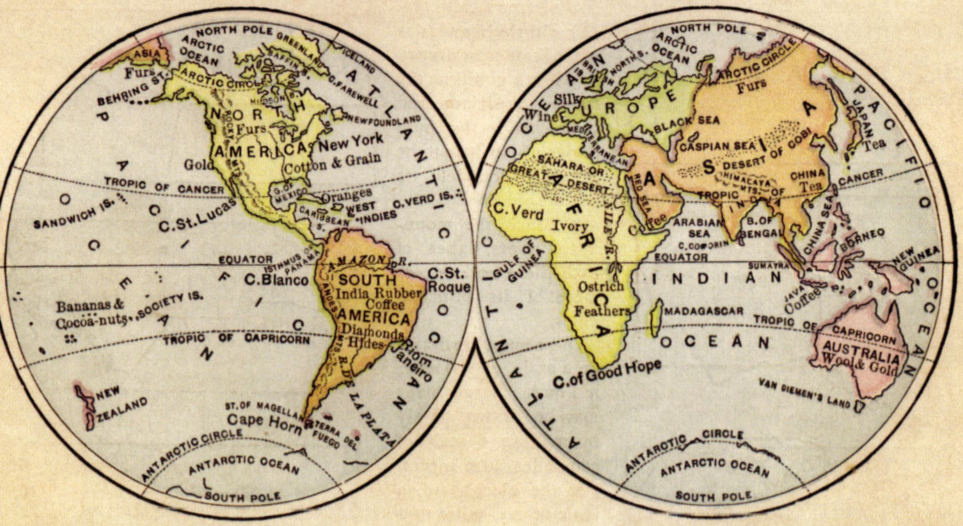

The Western Hemisphere

The Eastern Hemisphere

HEMISPHERES

If we looked at our planet from outer space, it would look like a huge blue ball. If we cut the ball in half from top to bottom, we would have hemispheres. Hemi means "half," and a sphere is round—so a hemisphere is half of something round. The Earth's Eastern Hemisphere includes Africa, Australia, Europe, and Asia. People who come from this part of the world sometimes call it the "Old World." The Western Hemisphere has what today we call the Americas. Once they found out it was there, people in the Eastern Hemisphere called the Western Hemisphere the "New World." But it wasn't new to the millions of people who had lived there for thousands of years.

The Western Hemisphere has two continents. One of them is South America. The second continent is North America. It includes Canada, the United States, Mexico, Central America, and the islands of the Caribbean Sea.

A few years after the Roosevelt Corollary was stated, a revolution began in the Central American country of Nicaragua. The country had a dictator named José Santos Zelaya.

The United States didn't like Zelaya. He was anti-American. He also was trying to control his neighbors. The United States wanted to be the only powerful country in the area.

Zelaya also had ties to Europe. He got loans from banks in Europe. The United States didn't like that either. Roosevelt wanted Europe out of the Western Hemisphere.

Nicaraguans didn't like Zelaya much either. In 1909, some of them took over part of the country. The United States helped. But Zelaya fought back. He captured some rebels and killed them.

The rebels eventually won. Adolfo Díaz became the president in 1911. The United States agreed to help him on one condition. He had to cut ties with Europe. He had to look to the United States for help.

Nicaragua was a colony of Spain until 1821. Many buildings in the country were made in a Spanish style.

The United States grew more and more powerful in Nicaragua. It took over the country's **trade**. It controlled the president.

Eventually, the United States military arrived. Zelaya's supporters were trying to take over again. The United States sent warships and marines in 1912. The marines stayed after the conflict ended.

Adolfo Díaz was president of Nicaragua twice, in the 1910s and again in the 1920s.

The battleship USS *Delaware* was one of the American warships sent to Nicaragua in 1912.

Haiti was another country where the United States had a lot of power. Haiti used to be a French colony. Slaves revolted and made Haiti a country in 1804. For a while, Haiti ruled itself. The people of Haiti didn't want other countries coming in.

By 1900, there were some Europeans who lived in Haiti's capital. They were mostly from Germany and France. A lot of them sold Haitian coffee to other countries.

France offered to help Haiti out with its money problems. The United States didn't like that at all. Remember, it wanted to keep Europe out of the Americas.

The United States started thinking more about Haiti. Eventually, it helped a new president get elected in Haiti. The president was controlled by the United States. And Haiti became another country where the United States had a great deal of control.

Mostly, the United States was thinking about getting more power in Latin America. But there was still the rest of the world. The United States wanted to be a world power. It set its sights on other countries, too, including China.

Once a slave, Toussaint L'Ouverture became a skilled military commander. He led the fight for Haiti's independence in the late 1700s and early 1800s.

Much of the fighting in China's Boxer Rebellion took place in the northeastern part of the country, including in the city of Tianjin.

European countries, as well as Japan, had a great deal of control over many areas of China. In 1900, Chinese people known as the Boxers revolted. However, European and Japanese armies were sent to China, and they put down the Boxer Rebellion.

Then, in the early 1900s, the Chinese government got some loans from German, British, and French banks. The money was for a railroad.

Again, the United States didn't like that. A group of American bankers offered to give China money instead. By 1909, China had two offers, from the Europeans and the Americans. It went with the Europeans.

Then, the United States put some pressure on China. The U.S. president, William Howard Taft, sent a note to the government of China's emperor, or leader. Taft let China know that the United States really wanted to give China money. China gave in, and in 1911, it accepted money from American banks.

The United States was gaining power through money. This policy was called "Dollar Diplomacy." Instead of just using the army to control other countries, the United States was using money.

Philander Knox, President Taft's secretary of state, helped create the Dollar Diplomacy policy.

American money helped China build a railroad from the Huguang region to the city of Canton, now called Guangzhou.

WILLIAM HOWARD TAFT

William Howard Taft was the 27th president. He was elected after Theodore Roosevelt.

Taft was the secretary of war under Roosevelt. He knew that Roosevelt wanted him to be the next president. Roosevelt was a popular president. People would vote for the man he wanted to come next.

Taft won the 1908 election easily. Then, he had to actually lead the country. He focused a lot on what was going on in Latin America. He pretty much continued Roosevelt's ideas and actions.

Taft wasn't very well-liked as a president. Lots of people disagreed with him. He served only one term as president. He later became the head of the Supreme Court. He is the only person to have been both the president and the chief justice of the Supreme Court.

GET THINKING

Wealth and Political Influence

The United States is a wealthy country. Sometimes, it has used its wealth to change the leaders of other countries or to push foreign governments to adopt certain policies. Should a country use money to influence another country's government? What are some other ways that one country could influence another nation?

The United States in Central America and the Caribbean

1 Nicaragua

During the late 19th and early 20th centuries, U.S. fruit companies forced Nicaraguan farmers from their land. The companies built huge farms. The Nicaraguan government, based in Managua, tried to stop the fruit companies, but it did not succeed.

2 Dominican Republic

Between mid-1902 and mid-1904, the Dominican Republic had four presidents. All of their governmwents were based in Santo Domingo. The United States interfered in all the elections to try to affect the outcome.

3 Haiti

Seven Haitian presidents were killed or overthrown between 1911 and 1915. The U.S. government worried about whether Haiti could stay **stable**. It also wanted to protect American sugarcane farmers there. U.S. soldiers landed in Port-au-Prince, the capital, to take over the country in 1915.

4 Panama

When Panama became an independent country, its capital was Panama City. Its leaders wrote a new **constitution**. This document allowed the U.S. government to send American soldiers into Panama.

LEGEND

Water	Caribbean	South America
Country Border	Central America	United States
Capital	Mexico	

Chapter Four

President Wilson

Woodrow Wilson was elected as the president in 1912. Changes were happening in Washington, D.C.

The United States kept getting stronger. It still wanted a presence all over the world. Wilson generally went along with the ideas of the two presidents who had come before him, Roosevelt and Taft. One of the places where Wilson got involved was Mexico.

The United States and Mexico share a long border. That doesn't mean they always get along. In the 1800s, the United States took a lot of land away from Mexico. The United States got bigger. Mexico got smaller.

By the end of the 1800s, the two countries were at peace, though. Porfirio Díaz was Mexico's leader until 1911. He wasn't a very good leader for the average Mexican. He treated Mexico's Native peoples badly. He gave away Mexican land. He also borrowed a lot of money from other countries.

Díaz made a lot of money for himself. He didn't let his people have much of it. Mexicans were unhappy.

Porfirio Díaz did not allow newspapers in Mexico to criticize him. He made sure his friends were elected to public office.

The Rio Grande in Texas forms part of the 1,950-mile (3,140-km) border between the United States and Mexico.

In 1910, a revolution broke out. In the Mexican Revolution, the poor and the **middle class** fought against the president. They won.

The rebels set up Francisco Madero as the president. But soon, the winners of the revolution were fighting with each other. They couldn't agree on how to run the government.

All those countries that had given Mexico money were worried. What would happen?

More changes were coming soon. Some people were unhappy with Madero. They wanted yet a different government. Those people got together. They chose Victoriano Huerta as their new president. Then, they killed Madero and made Huerta the leader of Mexico in 1913.

Under Porfirio Díaz's presidency, farming families in Mexico became poorer. They joined the Mexican Revolution, in which women fought alongside men.

That was where President Wilson came in. He took office as president in the United States at the same time Huerta did in Mexico. Wilson refused to say that Huerta's government was **legitimate**. Wilson thought that Huerta could easily become a dictator. Wilson wanted the people who had supported Madero to lead Mexico instead.

Francisco Madero wanted Mexico to be a democracy.

Soon, Huerta declared himself as a dictator. He had a lot of power. What's more, Wilson thought that Europeans were helping Huerta. President Wilson wouldn't stand for that. Pretty soon, the United States invaded Mexico.

Now there was fighting between Americans and Mexicans. Soldiers fought and died.

Huerta was in trouble. People who disagreed with him persuaded him to leave. But by now, the United States was committed to fighting. Americans couldn't back down now.

Victoriano Huerta resigned as president in 1914 and fled to Spain.

In 1915, Pancho Villa led an army in northern Mexico. This location made it easy for him to attack places in the United States.

The Americans eventually decided to support a man named Pancho Villa. He was on their side. He was connected to another man named Emiliano Zapata.

At first, the United States and Villa worked together. Then, things changed. In 1915, the United States decided to finally officially recognize the Mexican government. It supported Venustiano Carranza as president.

Villa was angry. He crossed into the United States and killed Americans. Soon, the United States struck back. It sent General John Pershing and more than 14,000 U.S. Army troops into Mexico to find him.

The general never found Villa. But the search grew and grew. Warships, airplanes, and border patrols got involved.

The whole thing was a mess. It had long-lasting effects on the United States and on Mexico. In Mexico, people didn't like the United States anymore. Because of the United States, Mexicans had died and the country was in chaos. Many people in Mexico didn't trust the United States.

A museum in New Mexico displays one of the planes used by the U.S. military to try to catch Pancho Villa.

REVOLUTIONARY HEROES

Pancho Villa and Emiliano Zapata are considered to be heroes by a lot of people. Villa is particularly famous.

Villa was born in Durango, Mexico. He lived on a ranch until he was 16. Then he shot his boss's son for bothering his sister. He ran away to avoid getting in trouble. He became a miner and also stole cattle for a living. He got bored, so he started robbing banks.

Villa got together a group of men. Together they were outlaws. The Mexican government was looking for him. But poor people loved him. He was a hero for them. He stole from the rich and gave to the poor. He was a Mexican Robin Hood.

Villa and his gang fought for Francisco Madero. They wanted him to be president. Americans came to fight with them.

Americans couldn't get enough of Pancho Villa. He was in the newspapers all the time. Filmmakers came to Mexico to make movies about him.

Zapata was born in Anenecuilco, Mexico. He became a local leader in his town. He started growing an army. It grew bigger and bigger, and it eventually overthrew Porfirio Díaz. Later, his army fought against Victoriano Huerta.

Zapata wanted to give back the land to ordinary people. His motto was Tierra y Libertad, which means "land and liberty." He fought for people's rights for many years.

Some people in Mexico today remember Zapata with murals, or paintings on the walls of buildings.

Mexico wasn't the only place with trouble for President Wilson. The islands of the Caribbean had problems too. Presidents Roosevelt and Taft had already gotten the United States involved in the area.

In 1913, the Dominican Republic was still having problems. So the United States came up with the "Wilson Plan." The plan called for elections in the Dominican Republic run by Americans. The United States would help the Dominicans with their money problems. And the United States military would run the Dominican Republic's army.

The Dominicans accepted. They didn't have a lot of choice. The Wilson Plan didn't really work, though. The Dominican president it helped elect was weak. The government fell apart.

The United States finally just invaded the Dominican Republic in 1916. It took over the government. In the capital city of Santo Domingo, the United States put in its own military government, which lasted for almost ten years.

Meanwhile, in another area of the Caribbean, the United States bought part of the Virgin Islands **archipelago** in 1917. The purchased islands had been owned by Denmark. The U.S. government agreed to pay Denmark $25 million for them. The United States had wanted these islands for a long time. They were a good place for military reasons. The islands allowed the United States to control access to the Panama Canal.

Santo Domingo is one of the oldest cities in the Caribbean, with churches and other buildings that were put up in the 1500s.

After the Mexican-American War, fought from 1846 to 1848, the United States gained **500,000 square miles** (1,300,000 sq. km) of Mexican land.

The Virgin Islands archipelago includes about **90 islands**.

The city of **Santo Domingo** was started by Spanish settlers in **1496**.

The Philippines is an archipelago on the other side of the world from the United States. Spain controlled the Philippines for more than 300 years. Then, when Spain lost the Spanish-American War in 1898, the United States took over the islands.

In 1916, President Wilson decided to let the people of the Philippines have more of a say in governing their country. He decided to give them independence, but only when their government was stable. This was a step in a different direction. Usually, the United States was trying to have more control over countries. In the Philippines, Americans were trying to give up control. However, the process took a long time. The Philippines did not become independent until 1946.

A lot was going in the United States during the early years of the 20th century. America was getting bigger. It was figuring out how to use its new power.

But soon Americans would have other things to worry about. The United States would have to focus on Europe for a while. World War I was about to begin.

Many people in the Philippines wanted the islands to be independent as soon as the Spanish-American War ended. From 1899 to 1902, thousands of U.S. troops fought against and defeated Filipino rebels.

World War I began in Europe in 1914, after an Austrian leader was shot. The United States entered the fighting in 1917.

Timeline

1901—Vice President Theodore Roosevelt becomes president when President William McKinley dies after being shot.

1903—Panama wins its independence from Colombia, and the United States starts to build the Panama Canal.

1904—President Theodore Roosevelt announces the Roosevelt Corollary.

1908—William Howard Taft is elected president.

1909—The Great White Fleet returns to the United States.

1900	1903	1906	1909

1913—Woodrow Wilson becomes president of the United States.

1917— The United States purchases some of the Virgin Islands from Denmark.

1912	1915	1918	1921

1910—The Mexican Revolution begins.

1914—The Panama Canal is finished.

1916—Pancho Villa makes his first raids across the border into the United States.

Quiz

TWO
Which two countries share the Caribbean island of Hispaniola?

ONE
In what year did President Theodore Roosevelt state the Roosevelt Corollary?

THREE
In what country did Spain first want to build a canal across Central America?

FIVE
What is the name for a country's policy of gaining power through the use of money?

FOUR
What are the two continents of the Western Hemisphere?

SIX
Who is the only person to have been both U.S. president and chief justice of the Supreme Court?

EIGHT
For how many years did Spain control the Philippines?

SEVEN
How many American troops looked for Pancho Villa?

NINE
In what year was the Panama Canal completed?

TEN
How much did the United States pay Denmark for what is now the U.S. Virgin Islands?

ANSWERS

ONE 1904 TWO Dominican Republic and Haiti
THREE Nicaragua FOUR North America and South America
FIVE Dollar Diplomacy SIX William Howard Taft
SEVEN More than 14,000
EIGHT More than 300 NINE 1914
TEN $25 million

Key Words

archipelago: a group of islands

colonies: countries or areas that are under the control of another country

constitution: a document containing the basic laws of a nation or area

corollary: a statement that is based on an earlier fact. The Roosevelt Corollary was based on the Monroe Doctrine.

democracy: a form of government in which people vote for their leaders

dictator: a ruler who has all the power in a country or area

empire: a group of countries or areas under the control of one leader or one country

fleet: a group of warships under one leader

legitimate: in keeping with what is right and legal

middle class: the group of people in a country or area who are neither rich nor poor

stable: steady and unchanging

trade: the exchange of goods between countries or areas

Index

LIGHTBOX

SUPPLEMENTARY RESOURCES

Click on the plus icon ⊕ found in the bottom left corner of each spread to open additional teacher resources.

- Download and print the book's quizzes and activities
- Access curriculum correlations
- Explore additional web applications that enhance the Lightbox experience

LIGHTBOX DIGITAL TITLES

Packed full of integrated media

VIDEOS

INTERACTIVE MAPS

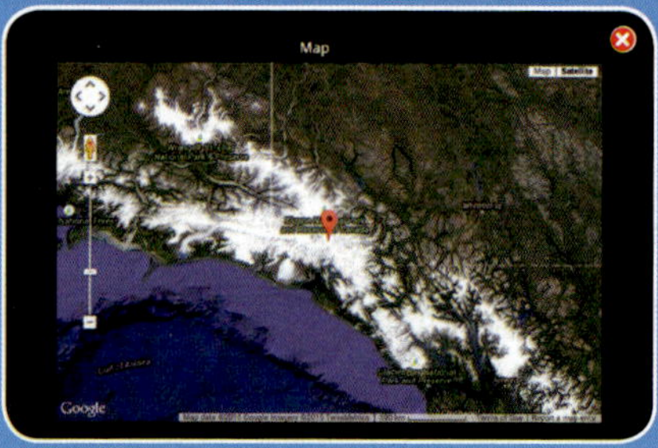

WEBLINKS

SLIDESHOWS

QUIZZES

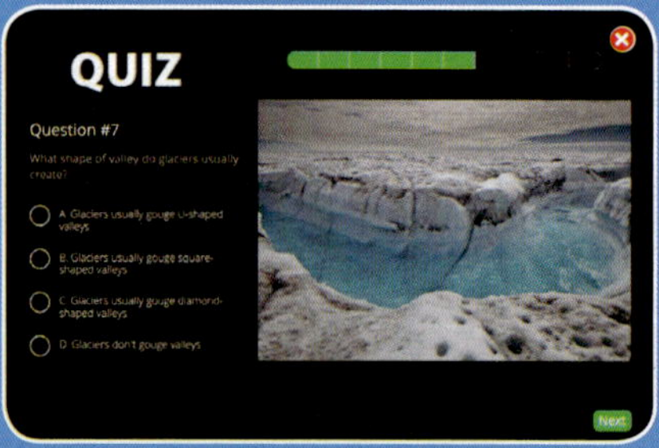

OPTIMIZED FOR

- ✔ TABLETS
- ✔ WHITEBOARDS
- ✔ COMPUTERS
- ✔ AND MUCH MORE!

Published by Smartbook Media Inc.
350 5th Avenue, 59th Floor
New York, NY 10118
Website: www.openlightbox.com

First published by Mason Crest in 2013

062018
121117

Library of Congress Cataloging-in-Publication Data
Names: South, Victor, author.
Title: A shifting role (1900/1912) / Victor South.
Other titles: A shifting role.
Description: New York, NY : Smartbook Media Inc., [2019] | Series: How America became America | Includes index. | Audience: Grades 4-6.
Identifiers: LCCN 2017054971 | ISBN 9781510536081 (hardcover : alk. paper) | ISBN 978-1-5105-3609-8 (multi-user eBook)
Subjects: LCSH: United States--Foreign relations--1901-1909--Juvenile literature. | United States--Foreign relations--1909-1913--Juvenile literature.
Classification: LCC E756 .S68 2019 | DDC 327.73009/04--dc23
LC record available at https://lccn.loc.gov/2017054971

Printed in Brainerd, Minnesota, United States
1 2 3 4 5 6 7 8 9 0 22 21 20 19 18

Project Coordinator Heather Kissock
Art Director Terry Paulhus

Photo Credits
Every reasonable effort has been made to trace ownership and to obtain permission to reprint copyright material. The publisher would be pleased to have any errors or omissions brought to its attention so that they may be corrected in subsequent printings.

The publisher acknowledges Getty Images, Alamy, Newscom, Dreamstime, Shutterstock, and iStock as its primary image suppliers for this title.